THE HIGHBACK
HOAX

A SNOWBOARD CONSPIRACY THEORY

NITKA MARGA

Cover and interior design elements and illustrations
by Soulbound Books LLC, created using Canva.

For permission requests, inquiries, or further information, please contact
Soulbound Books LLC at www.soulboundbooksinfo.com

Printed and bound by Amazon KDP
ISBN: 979-8-9891265-5-2

Dedication:

To all the riders who have come before us, carving out the history of snowboarding with each turn and jump, and to those yet to leave their mark on the slopes – this book is for you.

We mention names and brands within these pages – pioneers like Burton, legends like Tom Sims, and innovators like Halldor Helgason with Switchback Bindings. Each one has shaped the sport in their own unique way. But remember, they are just a few of the countless souls who have contributed to the evolution of snowboarding.

From the early board designers to the unsung heroes of the local shops, from the big-name competitors to the weekend warriors, each person has played a role in making snowboarding what it is today. And many more will continue to shape its future in ways we can't yet imagine.

This book, whether you find yourself nodding in agreement or shaking your head in debate, was crafted with you in mind – you brave, shredding souls. May it ignite discussions, spark memories, and inspire your next ride.

Enjoy, and keep carving your path in this incredible journey we call snowboarding.

Acknowledgment

As I embarked on the journey of writing "The Highback Hoax: A Snowboard Conspiracy," I embraced the support of artificial intelligence (AI) as an assisting tool. In an era of rapid technological advancement, AI has served as a valuable aid in the development of this book.

While AI has played a role in enhancing and refining the content, it's crucial to note that the core narrative, the essence of this story, originates from my personal experiences, creativity, and passion for snowboarding. AI's involvement has been that of a facilitator, helping to polish and organize my thoughts, rather than shaping the narrative itself.

I am grateful for this technological assistance, which has broadened my capabilities as a self-publishing author and enriched the overall reading experience. This book stands as a testament to the synergy of human imagination and technological innovation.

To you, the reader, thank you for your interest and support. It's my hope that this story resonates with you, reflecting the deep connection and love for snowboarding that inspired its creation.

With sincere thanks,
Nitka Marga

Contents

BREAKING POINT:
THE PROLOGUE

The dawn at Mt. Hood brought with it a canvas of nature's finest artistry. From the cozy confines of my tent, I glimpsed the peaks piercing the clouds, a sight that never failed to stir the soul. Beside me, Sheena, my trusty dog, lay peacefully, her presence a quiet reassurance in the wilderness. Outside, the day was already coming to life; Alex, ever the early riser, had a fire crackling, the aroma of breakfast in the air, and a Bloody Mary in hand, a nod to our unconventional mountain mornings.

Our refrigerator was a snow-buried cache, a testament to our improvised mountain life. This adventure was our bold leap after college—a month-long snowboarding escapade on Mt. Hood, followed by a road trip tracing the contours of California, eventually meandering back to our Colorado roots. It was more than a trip; it was a pilgrimage for freedom, for the unbridled joy of the ride.

Leaving the campsite that morning, we trudged towards Timberline Lodge, passing a caravan of makeshift homes on wheels—a collective of like-minded souls, each here for the mountain's call. The day on the board was exceptional.

The mountain offered a line of jumps, each a step higher, a challenge greater. The final leap, a 55-footer, beckoned. My confidence was sky-high; I had nailed backside 360s and 540s several times that morning, and now, the backside 720 on the largest jump was within grasp. Airborne, executing the maneuver, I felt invincible, shouting a triumphant "Yeeew!" to Alex, who was watching from the sidelines.

The landing, however, didn't follow the script. From a perfect touchdown to a disorienting tumble, I was suddenly on my back, sliding down the slope. The pain was absent at first, a numbness that gave way to a horrifying realization as I came to a stop: something was terribly wrong with my leg. The agony hit like a tidal wave, and consciousness slipped away.

Coming to, I found my head in Alex's lap, the world a blur of pain and confusion. Nausea overwhelmed me, and darkness took me again.

Each time I regained consciousness, it was a cycle of screams, tears, and the stark, jarring sight of my leg, grotesquely misshapen. Ski patrol was on its way, but each moment felt like an eternity.

Their arrival brought a mix of relief and dread; the journey down the mountain in the ski patrol's sled was an excruciating blur of bumps and jolts. In the ski patrol room, reality came crashing back as they began addressing my injuries. The first order of business was my boot, a fortress around the chaos of my broken leg.

As they reached for the boot, panic surged through me. My voice was a raw, desperate scream, "DO NOT FUCKING PULL THAT BOOT OFF!" Their hands paused momentarily, and one of them reassured me, "It's okay, we've got this." But they didn't understand.

"NO!" My scream was a mixture of pain and frustration. "Don't fucking do it!"

In that chaos, a younger ski patrol member, perhaps more attuned to the nuances of snowboard gear, stepped in. "Wait!" he intervened, halting his colleagues. "He's trying to tell us something." There was a brief, tense pause. "My inner laces are still tied. You're about to rip my leg off!" The words spilled out in a mix of agony and anger.

Acknowledging this, they cautiously worked to loosen the inner lacing system, a process that seemed to take an eternity. When I awoke again, my pants were cut open, and the boot was off. I caught a glimpse of my leg, a sight so shocking that my mind refused to retain it.

The next thing I remember is being in the ambulance. Clarity hit me the moment I saw the paramedics. Gritting my teeth, trying to communicate through the excruciating pain, I managed to utter, "I have no allergies. Drugs now, please."

As the drugs kicked in, a wave of relief washed over me. I called my parents in New Jersey, explaining that I had broken my leg and was headed to Portland. I reassured them that I would be receiving care from some of the best orthopedic surgeons. I even entertained the thought of returning to the campsite after getting a cast, not wanting to abandon our adventure. Handing the phone back to the paramedic, I heard him say, "If you have the means to fly out here, I highly recommend that you do so. Your son is safe, but he will need help."

As I closed my eyes in the ambulance, one question haunted me: "What the fuck happened?" I had landed the jump. Why did my leg break? That question is what brings us to this narrative and quest to challenge the status quo. This is a story of highbacks on snowboard bindings, a tale often untold and overlooked. But it's not just my story; this is our story, a story of every rider who's ever faced the unexpected consequences of what we've been sold as necessary gear.

Welcome to "The Highback Hoax: A Snowboarding Conspiracy Theory."

CHAPTER ONE:
THE FIRST
CARVES

In the early years of snowboarding, the sport was not just a novel pastime; it was a countercultural revolution. Born out of a desire to challenge the status quo, snowboarding emerged as a symbol of rebellion, an expression of freedom against the conventional and the expected.

The early pioneers of snowboarding were a diverse group of individuals drawn together by a shared passion for snow and the mountains. Many were influenced by the surf and skate cultures, seeking to bring that same sense of freedom and creativity to the snow-covered slopes. These trailblazers saw the potential for a new kind of sport, one that combined the fluidity of surfing with the agility of skateboarding.

In the beginning, the equipment was primitive and largely self-made. Boards were often simple, hand-crafted affairs, more akin to large, flattened surfboards than the sophisticated snowboards of today. Bindings, if they existed at all, were basic and often made from whatever materials were at hand. This DIY approach wasn't just a matter of necessity; it was a statement. These early riders were not just participants in a new sport; they were creators, innovators, and rebels.

The sport's early days were marked by experimentation and a constant reimagining of what was possible. Without the benefit of established techniques or equipment, these pioneers learned through trial and error. Every ride down the slopes was an opportunity to push boundaries and test new ideas. It was a time of rapid evolution, with each new season bringing fresh advancements and a deeper understanding of the sport's potential.

Snowboarding's appeal was its raw simplicity and the direct connection it offered with the natural world. In a time dominated by traditional winter sports like skiing, snowboarding stood apart. It was not just a different way to traverse snow; it was a different way to experience the mountain. Where skiers saw prescribed paths and structured techniques, snowboarders saw an open canvas, a space where they could carve their own lines and create their own style.

This spirit of innovation and nonconformity extended beyond the slopes. Early snowboarders often faced skepticism and even outright hostility from the established winter sports community. Ski resorts were slow to accept snowboarders, seeing them as a disruptive influence. But this resistance only strengthened the resolve of the snowboarding community. They didn't seek approval; they sought to redefine what it meant to be a winter athlete.

As snowboarding continued to grow, it began to attract attention beyond its core group of enthusiasts. The sport's unique style, combined with its ethos of freedom and self-expression, resonated with a wider audience. By the 1980s, snowboarding was beginning to move from the fringes of winter sports to the mainstream, but it retained its rebellious heart.

Looking back, it's clear that the early pioneers of snowboarding did more than create a new sport; they sparked a cultural movement. They challenged conventions, broke down barriers, and redefined what was possible on the snow. Their legacy is not just in the techniques they developed or the equipment they pioneered, but in the spirit of creativity and rebellion that continues to define snowboarding to this day.

As we delve deeper into the history of snowboarding, we must remember these early riders. Their courage, ingenuity, and passion laid the foundation for everything that followed. Snowboarding, as we know it today, owes its existence to their vision and determination. They were more than athletes; they were revolutionaries who changed the face of winter sports forever.

CHAPTER TWO:
HIGHBACK
REVOLUTION

As we navigate through paths of snowboarding history, we uncover a crucial chapter in its evolution: the introduction of the highback binding. This story, often untold yet pivotal, played a defining role in shaping the sport as we know it today.

In the early 1980s, a transformative idea took root. Snowboarding, still in its infancy, was ripe for change. Jeff Grell, a visionary in his own right, introduced the world to highback bindings, an invention that dramatically altered snowboarders' interaction with their boards and the mountain. The highback binding, first integrated into Flite snowboards and later adopted by other brands, offered unprecedented control and stability, especially on hardpack surfaces.

This era was marked by a flurry of innovation. Companies like Burton, Sims, and others were quick to recognize the potential of highbacks, incorporating them into their designs, each adding their unique twists and improvements. The 1990s saw Burton introducing freestyle bindings with injection-molded highbacks, further pushing the boundaries of what snowboarders could achieve.

However, behind the scenes of these technological advancements lay a deeper narrative, one of competition, collaboration, and perhaps, untold stories. The history of highbacks is not just a tale of innovation; it's a tapestry woven with threads of personal ambitions, market pressures, and the relentless pursuit of perfection.

As we acknowledge the contributions of pioneers like Grell and the efforts of companies like Burton and Flite, we also recognize that the full story might be more complex than the records show. Rumors and disputes, such as the contention over whether Grell or Louis Fornier first invented the highback binding, hint at a history not fully explored within these pages.

This chapter of snowboarding history serves as a reminder of the sport's dynamic and often competitive nature. It was a time of experimentation, where every new design and idea could lead to a breakthrough or a dead end. The pioneers of this era weren't just building snowboards; they were crafting a culture, a community, and, unknowingly, setting the stage for the controversies and conspiracies that would emerge later.

As we delve into the heart of our narrative — a conspiracy that threads through the fabric of snowboarding — understanding the history of highbacks becomes essential. It reveals a pattern of innovation shadowed by intrigue, of well-known achievements accompanied by lesser-known struggles. It shows us that in the world of snowboarding, as in many fields, the surface story is often just the tip of the iceberg.

CHAPTER THREE: THE SOUND OF STRAPS

Standing on a mountain, with the crisp, cool air brushing against my face, there's a sound that signals the start of an adventure, a sound as integral to snowboarding as the carving of snow itself. It's the slicing sound of my snowboard bindings securing my feet to the board, a reassuring confirmation that it's time to ride. For any rider, this sound is a call to freedom, a prelude to the rush that follows. It's a sound that has evolved over the years, mirroring the evolution of the sport itself.

In the early 1980s, snowboarding was still finding its feet, both figuratively and literally. Bindings in those days were basic, often just simple strap mechanisms or even makeshift solutions like rubber bands. They were rudimentary but crucial in providing the minimal connection between rider and board. However, as anyone who's tried to navigate a slope with such basic gear can attest, control was often more of a hope than a guarantee.

As the 1980s progressed, the snowboarding world began to witness a transformation in binding technology. Companies and individual innovators started experimenting with more secure and adjustable systems. This period marked the introduction of more sophisticated straps, offering better foot hold and control. These were not just incremental improvements; they represented a significant leap forward in the rider's ability to command the board.

Among the key players in this era of innovation was Jake Burton Carpenter and Burton Snowboards. While they weren't necessarily the first to introduce advanced strap-in binding systems, their role in refining and popularizing these systems cannot be understated. Burton's continual innovation in the design of straps and ladders helped shape the experience of strapping into a snowboard, making it more intuitive, secure, and effective.

However, it's important to also acknowledge the pivotal contributions of Tom Sims and Sims Snowboards. Tom Sims, a true pioneer of the sport, brought his own brand of creativity and innovation, significantly influencing the evolution of snowboarding equipment. His dedication to the development of snowboarding as a sport and lifestyle was instrumental in shaping its early days, from boards to bindings. Sims' contributions laid the groundwork for future innovations, helping to evolve snowboarding from a niche passion to a mainstream sport.

But the story of binding evolution isn't just about Burton or Sims. It's a narrative rich with contributions from numerous manufacturers, each bringing their own innovations and refinements. This era was marked by a collective push towards enhancing the snowboarding experience, with bindings being a focal point of this effort. As each manufacturer added their touch, the bindings became more than just a way to stay attached to the board; they became a critical component for control and performance.

Looking back, it's clear that the journey of snowboard bindings is deeply intertwined with the evolution of snowboarding itself. From those early days of makeshift setups to the sophisticated systems we see today, bindings have come a long way. They've transformed from being a mere necessity to an integral part of the snowboarding experience, enabling riders to push the limits of what's possible on a board.

As I stand here, ready to descend, I take a moment to appreciate this evolution. The sound of my bindings clicking into place is more than just a signal to start; it's a reminder of the journey this sport has taken, a journey marked by innovation, passion, and the relentless pursuit of improvement. And as I begin my descent, carving my path down the mountain, I'm not just riding on snow; I'm riding on the legacy of countless individuals who have shaped this sport into what it is today.

CHAPTER FOUR:
FALLING LEAF,
RISING SPIRITS

As a young ski and snowboard instructor, one of the first lessons I learned was the intricate dance of teaching. At 14, standing among seasoned instructors, my journey began with a humorous mix-up. My boss, mistaking me for one of the kids awaiting lessons, pointed me towards their table. But there I was, a young enthusiast eager to teach. His laughter, upon realizing his mistake, was a warm welcome into the world of instructing.

I started teaching skiing, the easier of the two disciplines to instruct, but it lacked the thrill and challenge of snowboarding. By 15, I made the switch to exclusively teach snowboarding, a decision that brought me two brothers as my first students. They were new to the sport, just a few years younger than me, and hungry to learn. They became my weekend companions for an entire season, a journey that would see them transform from novices to confident riders.

Our lessons began with the basics: understanding the gear, learning to balance with one foot strapped in, and navigating the gentle slopes of the magic carpet. But the real challenge, and the heart of our lessons, lay in mastering turns.

The difference between heel-side and toe-side turns is fundamental in snowboarding. Heel-side turns, where the rider leans back to press the heel edge into the snow, are more natural and intuitive. Most of us are accustomed to standing with weight on our heels, making this motion easier to adapt to.

In contrast, toe-side turns require a shift in balance that's less instinctive. Standing on your toes, or leaning into them while maintaining control and speed on a snowboard, is a challenging skill to master. To teach this, I introduced the brothers to the "falling leaf" technique on the bunny slopes. They first learned to glide down the slope on their heel side, swaying like a leaf in the wind. Once they were comfortable with that, we switched to toe-side.

Watching them struggle and then slowly gain control was a lesson in patience and perseverance, not just for them, but for me as their instructor. Each small victory, each successful turn was a step towards their mastery of the board. By the end of the season, the brothers were not just riding the slopes; they were owning them, confidently navigating rails and jumps in the terrain park (a little secret from our boss).

This journey of teaching and learning wasn't just about snowboarding techniques; it was about the nuances of balance, the physics of motion, and the joy of guiding someone through the discovery of their own potential. It underscored the unique challenges of snowboarding compared to skiing, the intricacies of movements that define the sport.

As we progressed through the season, it became clear how the evolution of snowboarding gear, particularly bindings, played a crucial role in enhancing these experiences. The advancements in binding technology, as discussed in the previous chapter, were not just about securing the rider to the board; they were about enabling these nuanced movements, these subtle shifts in balance that make snowboarding the exhilarating sport it is.

Reflecting on those days, the sounds of bindings clicking, the crisp mountain air, and the laughter of triumph over a newly learned trick, I realize how much snowboarding has given me. It's a sport that's as much about teaching and learning as it is about riding. It's about the connection we forge with our board, with the mountain, and with each other. As riders, we're constantly learning, evolving, and pushing the boundaries of what's possible on a snowboard, just like the sport itself has evolved over the years.

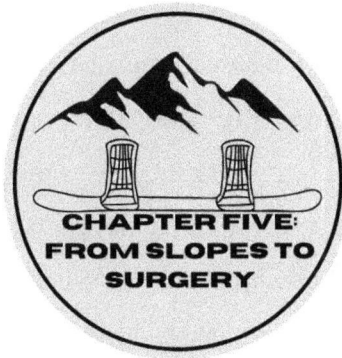

CHAPTER FIVE:
FROM SLOPES TO
SURGERY

The narrative takes a poignant turn as it revisits a defining moment in my life – an accident that reshaped my understanding of recovery and resilience. The year was 2013, and I found myself in an emergency room in Portland, a far cry from the snow-covered slopes and the thrill of snowboarding.

As they wheeled me into the ER, I was met with the curious, intense gazes of the medical staff. There was a mix of eagerness and professionalism in their eyes, a readiness to face the challenge that my injury presented. I could sense their intrigue as they peered at my leg, each nurse taking a moment to witness the spectacle of the injury. Strangely, this attention brought a sense of validation and safety. The drugs that coursed through my veins blurred the edges of my memory, but one detail remained crystal clear – the reassurances from nearly every medical professional who glanced at my mangled leg. They spoke of the hospital's reputation for having some of the best orthopedic surgeons in the world. People came from far and wide for their expertise. "You're going to make a full recovery," they said. To me, that meant getting back to the campsite, to the mountains, to snowboarding.

Yet, as I would soon discover, their definition of a "full recovery" was different from mine. They were talking about the ability to stand, to walk – a journey that would prove to be longer and more challenging than I could have anticipated.

The journey to the operating room was surreal. The sound of Notorious B.I.G. filled the hallways, the bass pulsing through the air, adding a strange yet badass soundtrack to the moment. The closer we got to the surgery room, the louder the music became. The brightly lit room was a stark contrast to the dark uncertainty that lay ahead. The rap music was turned down as a surgeon spoke through his mask, offering words that would stay with me: "We are stronger than we know. I'll see you in a couple of hours."

As I drifted into unconsciousness, lulled by the fading beats of Biggie's music, a mix of fear and trust battled within me. It was the beginning of a journey that would test not just my physical strength but the very essence of my spirit. It was a path that would lead me to confront the realities of recovery, the limitations of the body, and the indomitable strength of the human will. This chapter closes as I succumb to the anesthesia, the echoes of the surgeon's words a faint but steady beacon in the uncertain journey that lay ahead.

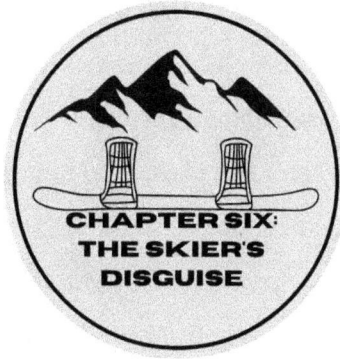

CHAPTER SIX:
THE SKIER'S
DISGUISE

The year is 2023, and I find myself in a peculiar yet familiar role – a custom ski boot fitter. It's a role that I play with a mix of amusement and professionalism. Yes, I can ski, and I do enjoy it, but deep down, I know the truth. I'm not really a skier at heart; I'm a snowboarder.

My journey in the ski and snowboard industry spans about 20 years. Over the years, that path through the ski and snowboarding industry has been varied and rich, touching almost every aspect of the business. I've worn many hats, each with its unique set of challenges and rewards. As a rental technician, I had the opportunity to introduce newcomers to the world of snow sports, guiding them in selecting the right equipment. In retail, I learned the art of matching the right gear with the right person, understanding the subtle differences in preferences and needs.

Managing ski shops allowed me to dive deeper into the business side of things – inventory management, customer service, team leadership, and the delicate balance of maintaining a profitable yet customer-focused operation. But of all the roles I've played, ski tuning was by far my favorite. There was something deeply satisfying about the meticulous process of tuning skis – the precise edge work, the careful waxing, and the art of ensuring each ski was in peak condition for the slopes. It was a role that married technical skill with a craftsman's touch, a perfect blend of science and art.

Now, I find myself in the world of boot fitting. While it's a different pace and focus compared to ski tuning, it has its own rewards. Custom fitting ski boots is a complex, nuanced process. It's about understanding not just the anatomy of the foot but also the individual's style and needs on the slopes. Each person's foot is a unique puzzle, and finding the perfect fit is both a challenge and a joy. Ensuring that a skier steps out with boots that offer comfort, performance, and precision is a responsibility I take seriously.

One day, a regular customer walks in, curious about what skis I'm using this season. I mention that I'm waiting for a new pair, courtesy of my boss – a truth that conveniently omits my primary preference for snowboarding. The conversation naturally drifts to my past, and I find myself revealing more than I usually do. I lift my pant leg to show the scar from my snowboarding accident years ago.

"Boot top fracture?" the customer inquires, eyeing the scar.

"Something like that, sir," I reply, with a half-smile, "spiral fractures, Tib, Fib, and Compartment Syndrome." At that moment, I wasn't really lying. The injury was indeed severe, a stark reminder of the risks inherent in snow sports, whether on skis or a snowboard.

The customer's innocent question unlocked a flood of memories, transporting me back to a Portland hospital room in 2013. There I was, lying on a sterile hospital bed, a stark contrast to the snow-covered slopes where I felt most at home. The walls of the room seemed to echo the seriousness of my situation, and the beeps of medical machines provided a rhythmic yet unsettling soundtrack.

In that room, I had an enlightening encounter with Dr. Smith, the surgeon who had skillfully navigated through the wreckage of my leg. He approached my bedside with a demeanor that was both professional and peculiarly warm. It was there that Dr. Smith decided to educate me, not just about my injury, but about a common skiing injury that my snowboarding accident had mirrored – the boot top fracture.

"Let me explain what a boot top fracture is," Dr. Smith began, his voice carrying a tone that was both instructive and gentle. "In skiing, it's a fracture that occurs just above where the rigid ski boot ends, typically involving the tibia. It's caused by the leverage force from the stiff boot during a fall." He paused for a moment, ensuring I was following along.

"Your injury, while similar in nature, is somewhat more unique than most," he continued. "You developed compartment syndrome, which adds another layer of complexity to your treatment."

I listened, fascinated and a bit overwhelmed. The way Dr. Smith described it made it clear – my snowboarding accident had resulted in an injury that was as severe as any boot top fracture experienced by skiers. The irony wasn't lost on me – a snowboarder learning about a skiing injury in the aftermath of an accident.

Dr. Smith, seeing my look of fascination mixed with apprehension, proceeded to explain the specifics of my treatment. "We've placed a rod and hardware to mend your bone," he said, detailing the intricate process of reconstructing my shattered leg. His explanation was clinical yet accessible, painting a clear picture of the steps taken to ensure my recovery.

Then, he delved into the topic of compartment syndrome. "It's a condition where pressure builds up in your leg, restricting blood flow and causing severe damage if not addressed promptly," he explained. The seriousness of this condition added another layer to the complexity of my situation.

As Dr. Smith spoke, I noticed a small hose protruding from the thick bandaging around my leg. "What's that, Dr.?" I inquired, my curiosity piqued despite the situation.

"That's helping to manage the pressure, bleeding, and fluids," he explained. "Right now, your leg is actually cut open from near your knee to near your ankle. We've filled it with a special spongy material that wicks away excess moisture and sends it through that hose into the bag beside your bed."

His words took a moment to sink in. "So, my leg is cut open?" I asked, trying to grasp the reality of it.

"Yes," he confirmed.

"Like, right now?" My voice was a mix of disbelief and a faint hint of humor, despite the gravity of the situation.

"Yes, right now," Dr. Smith replied. I looked down at my leg, wrapped and tubed, feeling detached from the severity of it all.

"I hardly feel it," I remarked, a wry smile forming on my face.

"That's because you're on a significant amount of medication," he said, a slight chuckle in his voice.

"Oh," I closed my eyes before continuing. "I feel that about me now."

CHAPTER SEVEN:
DISPELLING
MISCONCEPTIONS

As we delve deeper into this narrative, it's crucial to address a potential misconception. Some might think that I am gearing up to blame my highback bindings for the catastrophic leg break I experienced. Let me be unequivocally clear: this is not a crusade against highbacks. They were not the villains in my story.

This is a moment to pause and reflect. This tale is not just about an injury or a deep dive into snowboarding gear. It's a conspiracy, yes, but one that demands a nuanced understanding of the broader context. There's more to this story than meets the eye, or in this case, the leg.

We're embarking on a journey that explores the intricacies of snowboarding equipment, the evolution of the sport, and the interplay of various factors that contribute to both exhilaration and risk on the slopes. It's a multifaceted story, not reducible to a simple cause-and-effect.

Our aim is not to point fingers at a specific piece of equipment. Instead, we're peeling back the layers of a culture, a sport, and an industry. We're examining the decisions, designs, and developments that have shaped snowboarding bindings.

Every element in snowboarding, from the boots to the bindings to the board itself, plays a role in the dance between rider and mountain. This chapter reminds us that in the world of snow sports, and indeed in life, things are often more complicated than they appear. Yet, sometimes, they can also be much simpler – it often comes down to the art of noticing.

The breaking of my leg set me on an unexpected path, one that redefined my understanding of recovery and resilience. Embracing yoga, which aided my physical recovery, also brought a new dimension to my life. Since then, I've taught thousands of yoga classes, each one a step in my journey of healing and growth.

In the thick of it, recovery can feel like a low point, an endless struggle to find our way back. Sometimes, we might fail to recognize the complexity of our experiences that are, in fact, shaping us, molding us into more resilient beings. It's a complex process, but when viewed from a distance, it's inherently simple.

Let's consider a different exercise. Think about back pain, a common ailment affecting many. There are myriad causes, and each person's experience is unique. Yet, there's a simple concept underlying much of this pain that affects us all: our evolutionary history. Humans evolved from walking on all fours, and this transition, taking millions of years, has had a profound impact on our spines. This simple fact, when considered, can provide a new perspective on our individual experiences with back pain, highlighting how a complex issue can have straightforward underlying causes.

In the context of snowboarding and highback bindings, this perspective is key. Highbacks, like us, are part of their environment. They were created in response to the needs and demands of snowboarding, just as we adapt and grow in response to life. They are not the sole factor in my injury, nor in many snowboarding experiences. They are just one element in a complex interplay of factors – the rider, the gear, the environment, and the sport itself.

CHAPTER EIGHT:
THE HIGHBACK
DEBATE

The genesis of this chapter unfolded just days ago, stemming from an enlightening conversation with my roommate, who is also my boss at the ski boot fitting shop. He's a man of conviction, unyielding in his beliefs and quick to dismiss ideas he finds lacking merit. It's a trait I've come to admire for its honesty and directness. On this particular day, I found myself in a rare position – I managed to sway his firmly held beliefs about snowboarding bindings.

As he walked into our condo in Jackson, he caught me in the midst of what could only be described as a research session with my snowboard and boots. I was deep in thought, contemplating the necessity of highbacks on snowboard bindings. He was quick to challenge my musings. "Sure, if you don't want heel side edge response," he retorted confidently. His stance was clear: removing highbacks would diminish a snowboard's responsiveness, particularly on the heel side.

I urged him to step into my snowboard bindings, which were laid out on the carpet among an array of ski and snowboard gear. Our conversation continued, him advocating for the inevitable shift of snowboarders to plastic shell snowboard boots, me arguing that while such boots might be beneficial for extensive touring with a split board, they were hardly necessary on the slopes. In fact, I ventured, highbacks themselves might not be as crucial as we've been led to believe.

All the while, he unconsciously rocked back and forth on my snowboard, unique with it's no highbacks. His sneakers, loosely strapped under the snowboard binding straps, allowed his feet to move considerably. Yet, I noticed something telling in his movements. While he easily rocked back, lifting his toes and leaning into his heels, not once did he shift his weight forward to lift his heels off the board. It was a natural, effortless motion to rock back, but moving forward required deliberate effort, a conscious decision.

I paused our debate, pointing out this observation. "Dude, this entire time we've been speaking, you have been effortlessly moving to your heels, but not once did you move to your toes and lift your heels." There was a moment of silence as the realization set in. It didn't take much more for him to grasp the implication of what he'd been unwittingly demonstrating.

"But, wait," he finally said, "You want the responsiveness the high back provides. That tight plastic response, like a ski boot."

"John, focusing so much on one direction doesn't really match up with snowboarding's whole-body movement. Skiing's mechanics might be a different story. I'm no physicist, but I know snowboarding – our feet are connected on the same plane, we have two less edges, our hips face a different direction, and our movements are varied. It's not the same as skiing."

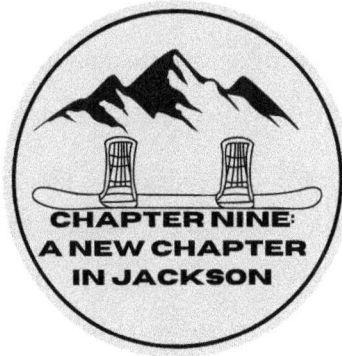

**CHAPTER NINE:
A NEW CHAPTER
IN JACKSON**

The early light of dawn cast a soft golden glow over Jackson Hole Mountain Resort, painting a breathtaking picture that starkly contrasted with the familiar slopes of New Jersey, a place I proudly called home. There, on the modest yet cherished runs, I honed my skills, seizing every opportunity to ride. My snowboarding sessions only ceased when the spring sun transformed the snow into mud, signaling a transition to a different kind of thrill: dirt biking. These slopes, while not as vast as those in Colorado or Wyoming, held a dear place in my heart.

Standing in Teton Village, a surge of emotions enveloped me. This marked my return to the Rockies after five years – years filled with life's intricate tapestry of experiences, from running a yoga studio to navigating the ebbs and flows of personal challenges. Here in Jackson Hole, I stood on the brink of a new chapter, ready to intertwine the lessons of my past with the adventures of my snowboarding journey ahead.

The cold Wyoming air filled my lungs as I gazed out at the peaks from the top of the tram, silent sentinels to the tales of every skier and rider who had dared their paths. As I prepared to etch my own story into these slopes today, my mind was a mosaic of memories from New Jersey's runs and Colorado's canyons. Alongside these recollections were lessons gleaned from yoga and the unwavering support of family and friends. Each turn and descent I was about to undertake stood as a testament to my enduring passion for the sport, a constant echo of where my journey began and how far I had traveled.

The crisp mountain air filled my lungs as I fastened my front binding, unique in their lack of highbacks, I skated towards the edge. These bindings, companions to hundreds of days on the slopes over the past decade, stood as a testament to my ongoing experiment with snowboarding biomechanics. For over twenty years, I've been refining this practice, delving deep into the nuances of movement and balance on a board. Today marked not just a return to the slopes but a continuation of my lifelong journey to master the intricate dance between snowboarder and snow.

Before I dropped in, I found myself reflecting on the path that led me to this point. Departing from Colorado, a place that had been my home for a decade, was a decision fraught with complexity. There, I had crafted a life rich in experiences and connections. Yet, the pull towards a new beginning was undeniable. In 2018, I answered this call, returning to my roots in New Jersey, where I embarked on a new venture: opening a yoga studio.

That studio became a vessel for my passion, witnessing over two thousand classes, serving as a sanctuary during the tumultuous times of a global pandemic, and shaping countless personal relationships. Each class taught, every challenge faced, and every bond formed or faded played a part in steering me toward this very moment, high above the slopes of Jackson Hole, ready for the next chapter.

I strapped into my back binding, my heart pounding with excitement and anticipation. This wasn't just a winter sabbatical or an escape from the norm; it was a quest for something deeper, a desire to reconnect with a part of me that I had left behind in Colorado. The mountain before me was not just a physical landscape; it was a canvas for my expression, a place where I could test my limits and explore the bounds of my capabilities.

As I made my first descent, I was acutely aware of every movement, every shift in weight, and every turn. Snowboarding has always been a dynamic dance for me, a harmonious blend of strength, flexibility, and intuition. I remembered my years as a yoga instructor, how I taught others to be mindful of their bodies, to move with intention. Now, I applied those lessons to myself, feeling the board respond to my every command.

Carving down the mountain, I felt a sense of liberation. Here, amidst the towering peaks and sprawling white slopes, I found clarity. My legs moved with precision and grace, not once constrained by the absence of highbacks. I charged through the groomers, weaving between trees, feeling every contour of the snow beneath me. It was exhilarating, a reminder of why I fell in love with this sport so many years ago.

But it was more than just the thrill of the ride. As I pushed my body to its limits, I realized that the true response and control I sought came from within. It was in the way my muscles tensed and relaxed, the way my ankles flexed and pivoted, the way my body intuitively knew how to balance and maneuver. The highbacks, I realized, were never the source of my stability or control; it was always me, my body, and my connection to the board.

By the time I reached the bottom of the slope, I knew I had re-discovered something profound. This was not just a return to snowboarding; it was a reawakening, a realization that the power I sought on the slopes had been with me all along.

In Jackson Hole, I had found more than just a new home – I had found a deeper understanding of myself, both as a snowboarder and as a person.

THE HIGHBACK
HOAX
INTERMISSION

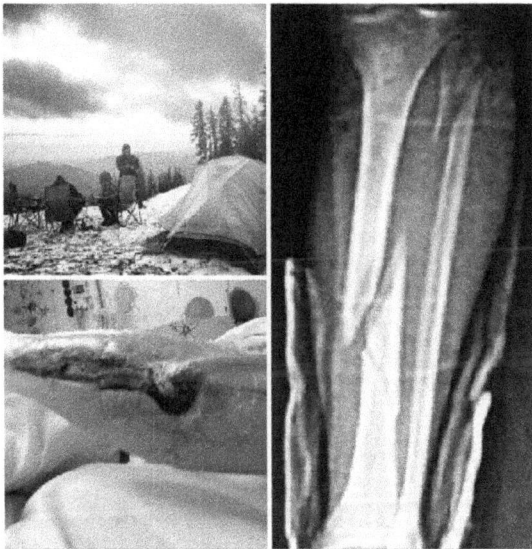

So, we'll give 'em the strap replacements... at a charge of course. And we wont offer highback replacements.

I know what you're thinking, sir. What if they just take their highbacks off. We've thought of that. You can't take the highback off. Its the same hardware that holds the strap.

We shall forge a power so dark, so absolute, that the very mountains shall bend beneath our might. By the edge of the twisted blade and the howl of the storm, the slopes shall be ours, and the snow shall heed our command. The realm of winter will tremble at our feet, and from the highest peak to the deepest valley, all shall know our rule!

**CHAPTER TEN:
A LIVING
LEGEND**

And now, we introduce a legend...

An architect of aerial artistry...

Master of the mountains, conqueror of the cold...

Revolutionary, reshaping my experience of snowboarding...

A Dutchman with an indomitable spirit...

In the snowboarding world, Halldór Helgason stands out as a multifaceted icon. More than just a competitor with X Games medals, he has deeply influenced snowboarding culture. His presence is felt across various formats – from high-profile films to countless video projects and online content. To truly grasp his impact, one should delve into his extensive portfolio, where his versatility shines in park, street, powder, and competitive scenes. Halldór embodies the spirit of snowboarding, merging athletic prowess with artistic expression. His journey isn't just about the accolades but the story he tells through every ride, every film, and every turn.

In 2013, a few short months before I would experience a life-altering injury, Denver was alive with the energy of the annual ski and snowboard convention. This year's event saw me interning for Grenade Gloves. Amid industry legends like Danny Kass and The Dingo, my days were a blend of assisting with presentations, networking with potential buyers, and immersing myself in the snowboarding culture, unaware of the dramatic turn my path was about to take.

Beyond the professional facade, the convention was a melting pot of après-ski culture. With about 30% of my time dedicated to work, the remaining hours were an exhilarating blend of camaraderie and revelry. From sharing drinks in hidden corners of company booths to seeking VIP access to the most anticipated after-parties, every moment pulsed with the spirit of snowboarding.

One memorable night, our Steamboat crew, ever on the lookout for adventure, scored tickets to a coveted after-party. As The Misfits played, we embraced the moment with an impromptu beer-spraying celebration on the dance floor. It was a wild scene, embodying the freedom and rebellion synonymous with snowboarding culture. However, our enthusiasm led to a swift ejection from the venue.

Outside, amidst rolling laughter and burning joints, we unexpectedly found ourselves in the company of Halldór Helgason. He too had been caught up in the excitement and found himself ousted alongside us. I remember him vividly, holding his neck with his hands, still reeling from the neck injury sustained at the X-Games just days before. It was a stark reminder of the risks and realities of our sport. The night was far from over. With a collective decision to keep the party going, we set off for the next destination, a strip club where Tech Nine and The Gremlinz were said to be hosting. Halldór generously offered to cover the cab fare, but we opted to walk, valuing the opportunity to spend more time with one of our idols. Our journey through Denver was an eclectic mix of pit stops, laughter, and shared experiences, with Halldór's spirit shining through despite his recent ordeal.

The walk through Denver was surreal. We stopped at an ATM for cash, then grabbed a bite at McDonald's, all the while with Halldór cradling his neck. The conversation flowed effortlessly among us, spanning from snowboarding tales to life's stories. Halldór's resilience and down-to-earth demeanor added depth to our understanding of him, not just as a snowboarding icon but as a person who embodied the essence of our sport.

That night in Denver wasn't just about partying. It was a profound testament to the snowboarding community – a group defined by its resilience, camaraderie, harmless rebelion, and an unwavering passion for life. For me, it was a moment of realization, an acknowledgment of the shared spirit that binds us all in the snowboarding world.

Sitting in a Denver strip club, next to Lucas Magoon as he playfully slapped a tower of dead presidents onto the stage, I viewed snowboarding as much more than a sport. It's a way of life, a somewhat kind and somewhat reckless path, a wild journey. Sometimes, that journey means celebrating the unexpected, like spraying beer to the surprise tunes of The Misfits spun by a DJ.

**CHAPTER ELEVEN:
THE EVOLUTION OF
FORWARD LEAN IN
SNOWBOARDING**

The introduction of forward lean in snowboard bindings was a pivotal development in the sport's evolution. Initially, bindings had basic straps that, while securing the feet to the board, didn't offer the precise and snug fit necessary for advanced maneuvers. This was the backdrop against which forward lean emerged in the late 1980s to early 1990s, primarily to cater to aggressive riders who sought to enhance their toe-side turns.

However, the focus on forward lean brought to light a critical aspect of snowboarding dynamics. The sport isn't merely about linear forward and backward movements. Snowboarding involves a complex interplay of angles and body shifts. As a rider carves and turns, the orientation of their feet, hips, and entire body undergoes constant change, challenging the notion that responsiveness is only needed in the forward and backward directions.

The introduction of forward lean coincided with a time when carving and making big turns were considered almost as challenging as tricks. This feature was designed to help riders maintain a more aggressive stance, crucial for making these dynamic moves. But this development also highlighted a gap in binding technology. The need for equipment that could support the dynamic, multi-directional nature of snowboarding was becoming increasingly apparent.

Snowboarding's growth and its community's evolving demands led to further advancements in binding technology. Straps became more sophisticated, offering better fit and control. The design and functionality of bindings continued to evolve, with manufacturers experimenting with different materials, shapes, and configurations to enhance rider experience and safety.

CHAPTER TWELVE:
THE HIGHBACK'S
TALE - A
SNOWBOARDING
RAP

Yo, let's rewind, back in time, to snowboarding's early climb,

Highbacks rose, dominating the grind,

Straps were basic, not yet in their prime,

Bindings evolving, but highbacks, still the headline.

Highbacks in the game, standing tall through the years,

As bindings changed, they calmed riders' fears,

Straps got stronger yo, boots hugged tight,

Yet highbacks remained, a familiar sight.

Tech advanced, bindings got a new face,

But highbacks stayed, held their place,

Not just relics, they adapted the pace,

In the evolution race, they made their case.

Bindings transformed, but one thing stayed true,
Highbacks persisted, part of the crew,
Evolution's tale, complex and wide,
Highbacks witnessed, never left the ride.

In this rap, we question, reflect, and see,
Bindings changed, but what about the highback's legacy?
An emblem of past, or still a key?
In snowboarding's story, they're part of the spree.

This rhyme's a journey, through tech and time,
Exploring bindings, in rhythm and rhyme,
Highbacks' role, in the modern day gear,
A question we ponder, in the snowboarding sphere.

CHAPTER THIRTEEN: THE TALE OF TWO BINDINGS

In a factory humming with the rhythmic dance of machines, a new snowboard binding was being born. From a complex, intricately designed mold, it emerged, a testament to the precision and innovation that defined its creation. Each part, from the sturdy baseplate to the sleek highback, was assembled with meticulous care, blending form and function into a seamless whole.

The binding's first journey was not down a snowy slope, but rather, it traveled from the factory's secure embrace to the bustling world of a company rep. There, among its kin, it awaited the call of the mountains, eager for the embrace of a snowboard and the snug fit of a boot. It dreamt of snowy peaks and frosty trees, of the rush of cold air and the thrill of the descent.

When finally united with its board and boots, the binding felt complete. Together, they ventured to the mountains, where seasons of joy awaited them. The binding learned the language of the snow, from the gentle whispers of fresh powder to the harsh shouts of icy trails. It learned the rhythm of its rider, responding to their every move with steadfast loyalty. They carved paths down slopes, soared over jumps, and danced through every turn and twist the mountains offered.

But time, as it does, wore on the binding. The once shiny highback, a proud flag on the battlefield of snow, began to show signs of wear. And then, on a day like any other, in the midst of a bold, breathtaking descent, it happened. A snap, a break – the highback gave way. The binding's journey, it seemed, had come to its end.

Returned to its makers, the binding was laid out, a subject of both scrutiny and nostalgia. It was revealed to be a prototype, a forerunner of a new era in binding design. A virtual meeting was called, connecting the creators with the rider who had given this binding its life of adventure. Memories were shared, tales of snowy escapades exchanged, and a bond of mutual respect and affection acknowledged.

In the end, a decision was made. Inspired by this prototype, a new line of bindings would be launched, each aspiring to capture the essence of what made this one so special. The binding's legacy was to live on, not just in memory, but in the very design of future generations of snowboarding gear.

Yet, for this binding, the journey was over. It was time to be recycled, its components destined to be reborn in new equipment. In this cycle of creation, use, and rebirth, the binding found its eternal place in the ever-evolving story of snowboarding – a tale of innovation, adventure, and the relentless pursuit of riding the edge of possibility.

In another factory, under the same hum of machinery, a different binding is born. This one follows a path parallel to the first, journeying from the assembly line to the mountainside. It too forms an unbreakable bond with its rider, dancing through snow and air with grace and agility.

This binding was different. It had the usual ladder straps and heel cups, but its unique feature was the easily removable highback. A design that allowed riders, myself included, to choose their style, even mid-mountain. Over the years, many, like me, preferred to ride without the highbacks, finding a new sense of freedom and connection with the board.

Unlike its predecessors, this binding doesn't meet an early demise. Instead, it endures season after season, a relentless companion in the snowboarder's quest for adventure. Its durability catches the attention of the manufacturers.

In a decisive meeting, Halldor Helgason, the snowboarding maestro himself, appears on the screen. "Switchback Bindings," he announces with a nod of approval. Not a strap out of place, not a highback broken. The decision is unanimous – this binding, robust and unyielding, will be the blueprint for a new line, a testament to endurance and reliability in the demanding world of snowboarding.

**CHAPTER FOURTEEN:
THE DISAPPEARANCE
OF SWITCHBACK
BINDINGS**

The morning sun barely crept through the curtains as I reached for my phone, only to be greeted by an unexpected text from Ben. His message carried a tone of urgency, a concern that resonated with me instantly. "Switchback Bindings might be no more," it read. My heart sank a little. Ben and I, avid snowboarders, had been loyal to Switchback Bindings for years, specifically for their no highback design that suited our riding style perfectly.

"What happened?" I texted back, my mind racing with possibilities. The thought of losing access to these bindings was more than just a minor inconvenience; it felt like losing a piece of our snowboarding identity.

Ben's reply came quickly, "I have no idea. Maybe they didn't sell enough?" It was a plausible theory. In a market driven by constant innovation and frequent purchases, a product that lasts might paradoxically be at a disadvantage.

"That's crazy! Their bindings are awesome. I am a huge fan!" I replied, my fingers moving swiftly over the screen. It was the truth. Those bindings had been a game-changer for me, offering exactly what I needed – quality straps, sturdy heel cups, and the freedom of riding without highbacks.

"Yeah, but it's been like 9 years since you bought a pair. Maybe they're too good," Ben speculated. He had a point. In all these years, I hadn't needed to replace them, thanks to their durability and performance. It was a testament to their quality, but perhaps also a business challenge – how do you sustain sales when your product doesn't necessitate frequent replacements?

Our conversation drifted to what this meant for us as riders. The prospect of returning to highbacks or switching to step-in bindings didn't appeal to us. We craved the feel of stiff boots, the security of reliable straps, and the simplicity of a binding that perfectly complemented our riding.

As the day unfolded, I found myself pondering the fate of Switchback Bindings. Their potential disappearance from the market wasn't just a loss of a product; it was a challenge to a style of riding we had come to love. It raised questions about the snowboarding industry's direction and what it meant for riders like us, who valued functionality and longevity over the latest trend.

Unwilling to accept defeat, I decided to take action. I started by reaching out to other riders in our community, gauging their experiences and opinions on Switchback Bindings. The responses were varied but echoed a similar sentiment – a respect for the brand and what it offered. It became clear that these bindings weren't just equipment; they were part of a culture, a statement of snowboarding style and philosophy.

This chapter marked the beginning of a new quest – to understand the disappearance of Switchback Bindings and what it signified in the broader context of snowboarding culture. It was a journey that would take me beyond the slopes, into the heart of the snowboarding industry, where innovation, market demands, and rider preferences converged in a complex dance. As I delved deeper, I was determined to find answers and, hopefully, a way to keep the spirit of what Switchback Bindings represented alive in the snowboarding community.

CHAPTER FIFTEEN:
THE ROAD TO
RECOVERY AND
BEYOND

The chapter unfolds with a heartfelt scene at Timberline Lodge's Ski Patrol offices. At my side, my parents, carrying cases of beer. We stepped in to express my gratitude to the team that had swiftly come to my aid on the slopes of Mt. Hood. Their prompt assistance and care were my lifelines during one of the most challenging episodes of my life.

Transitioning to New Jersey in 2013, I'm back at my parents' house, which becomes my sanctuary of healing. My personal belongings are still in Colorado – a car, an apartment, remnants of a life momentarily on hold. Here, surrounded by family, I navigate through the nuances of recovery, a journey that proves to be both trying and transformative.

The montage continues, depicting the long and often frustrating path of healing. For four months, I am confined to a boot and crutches, each doctor's visit seeming to extend the timeline of my convalescence. The routine becomes all too familiar – go to the doctor, hear the same advice, and return in a month.

A pivotal change occurs with a second opinion. A new doctor questions the presence of crutches, leading to a moment of confusion, then clarity. Contrary to previous advice, she insists that the rod in my leg – a potentially permanent fixture – is robust enough to bear weight. It's crucial for my leg to endure some pressure to promote bone growth and healing. This revelation marks a significant shift in my recovery process.

Fueled by this new understanding, I leave the crutches behind and embrace a more active phase of healing. Returning to Steamboat Springs that winter, I cautiously but determinedly got back on my snowboard. I rode, mostly alone, on cat-tracks, practicing my switch abilities, careful yet eager to test my leg's limits, choosing to forgo highbacks for a sense of freedom and adaptability.

This return to snowboarding is a reflection of my journey back to health – each glide and turn mirrors the resilience of a recovering leg. The subsequent year, driven by a resolve to validate my leg's restored strength, I set out to conquer a new challenge – running a marathon. This endeavor transcends physical achievement; it symbolizes a victory over adversity, a celebration of recovery.

This chapter in my life, marked by a harrowing injury and the ensuing journey of recovery, is a narrative of unyielding perseverance. It underscores the capacity to overcome, to find strength in adversity, and embodies the indomitable spirit of not just a snowboarder, but a person who refuses to be defined by a single moment, no matter how defining it may seem.

In this journey, the kindness and expertise of so many have been a beacon of hope and strength. I extend my heartfelt gratitude to the nurses, doctors, physical therapists, EMTs, and all the healthcare professionals who dedicate their lives to helping others. Their commitment and compassion are the unsung melodies that harmonize the chaos of unexpected life events.

Special thanks also go to those who, in seemingly small but profound ways, contribute to the healing of others. Like the two young women I met in a liquor store in Government Camp– a chance encounter that left a lasting imprint on my heart. There I was, a disheveled figure on crutches, clad in oversized clothing from a Portland thrift store, an embodiment of my tumultuous state.

Their genuine inquiry about my injury led to sharing my foiled plans – a month of snowboarding and camping around Mt. Hood, followed by a road trip through California, ending back in Colorado. When I revealed the unfortunate twist of fate that occurred on my first day riding Timberline Lodge, their response was not just one of sympathy, but of uplifting encouragement.

Their gesture of kindness – a kiss on the cheek, a warm hug, and words whispered with empathy – resonated deeply. "We are stronger than we know," one of them murmured, echoing the very words spoken by my surgeon. In that moment, their simple act of human connection and encouragement felt like a guiding star, a reminder that strength often lies hidden within us, waiting to be acknowledged and embraced.

This chapter, while defined by physical recovery, is ultimately a narrative about the power of human connection, resilience, and the unwavering spirit of compassion that weaves through our lives. It's a reminder that every person we encounter – whether for a moment or a lifetime – plays a part in our story, and we in theirs, in ways we may never fully comprehend.

To all those who have crossed my path, whether in the corridors of hospitals, on the snow-covered slopes, sweaty-heated yoga studios, or in unexpected places like that liquor store near Mt. Hood – thank you. Your kindness, support, and belief in the strength that resides within each of us have been the undercurrents that propelled me forward, reminding me that indeed, we are stronger than we know.

**CHAPTER SIXTEEN:
UNRAVELING THE
CONSPIRACY**

In 2023, amidst the weaving of this narrative, a curious incident occurred. I reached out to Lobster Snowboards, intrigued by a binding in their catalog that strikingly resembled the Switchback binding - a design I had revered and relied on for years. This seemingly innocuous observation was the catalyst for a deep dive into a series of conspiracies surrounding the snowboarding industry.

Hi,

Thank you for reaching out! The highback can be removed on the Crusher binding and will be able to be ridden without them. Hope this helps!

The first thread of this intricate web involved the fate of Switchback Bindings. These bindings, praised for their durability and design, somehow couldn't sustain as a standalone company. It was a peculiar case in business where the product was so robust and long-lasting that its primary market rarely needed replacements. Was it possible that their excellence led to their downfall?

The journey of bringing a binding to market is a colossal endeavor, filled with challenges from mold creation to prototyping to marketing. The theory emerged that Lobster Snowboards, perhaps seeing an opportunity, acquired Switchback's molds. This move would allow them to benefit from Switchback's innovative design while circumventing the hefty initial investment.

Then the narrative took a darker turn, delving into the idea that major manufacturers in the snowboarding industry were conspiring against the concept of no highback bindings. The highback had become such a staple in binding design that its absence threatened the established order, potentially impacting the sales and market differentiation strategies of these large companies.

As the theories unraveled, a more profound conspiracy came to light. It wasn't just about the survival of a binding design or the preferences of manufacturers. The real issue was the snowboarding industry's apparent stagnation, its resistance to embrace newcomers and innovation. Even a figure like Halldor Helgason, a legend in the snowboarding world, faced obstacles in bringing a fresh perspective to the market. His success with Switchback Bindings, despite being a significant achievement, remained unknown to many.

This revelation pointed to a deeper problem – a snowboarding culture that had somehow lost its way, becoming insular and resistant to change. The essence of snowboarding, once defined by rebellion, creativity, and progress, seemed to have been overshadowed by commercial interests and a reluctance to evolve.

In a dramatic twist, the narrative circles back to the original point of contention - the necessity of highbacks in snowboarding. The conclusion is clear: with the advancement in boot and binding technology, highbacks are not a necessity for experienced riders. They might have served a purpose in the past, but the evolution of gear has rendered them more of a choice than a requirement.

The real conspiracy, it seems, is not just about the bindings themselves but about the industry's attitude towards innovation and change. It's a call to the snowboarding community to rekindle the spirit of evolution and openness that once defined the sport. This chapter serves as a reminder and a challenge - to look beyond the established norms, to question, and to embrace the possibilities of what snowboarding can become.

**CHAPTER SEVENTEEN:
THE HIGHBACK
PARADOX**

As I delved into the array of top-selling snowboard bindings, a pattern began to emerge, painting a picture of an industry at a crossroads. On one side, there was a clear emphasis on highbacks, with manufacturers showcasing innovations and advancements in highback technology as key selling points. On the other, there was a growing trend towards step-in bindings, touting convenience and speed as their primary allure.

However, this dichotomy revealed a deeper issue within the snowboarding community – a reluctance to embrace change that truly matters. The highback, once a revolutionary introduction to snowboarding gear, has now become a standard feature, one that manufacturers continue to tweak and market as a significant differentiator. But is this focus on highback technology genuinely reflective of the needs and desires of riders? Or has it become more about perpetuating a cycle of superficial upgrades for the sake of marketability?

The conspiracy, or perhaps more accurately, the symptom of a larger problem, becomes apparent. The industry, in its pursuit of innovation, seems to be overlooking what riders genuinely seek – quality, durability, and true advancements that enhance the riding experience. The fixation on highback technology, while it sometimes has its merits, often overshadows the potential for real evolution in binding gear design.

Ironically, the highback often becomes the first component to break on a binding, raising questions about its real necessity and durability. In stark contrast, my experience with Switchback Bindings paints a different picture. These bindings have impressively endured ten seasons, eight of which included over 100 days of riding each. As a ski tuner, I rode every day, rigorously testing these bindings. Their remarkable durability and consistent performance without highbacks underscore that we can achieve enhanced riding experience and longevity without relying solely on conventional design elements.

Yet, the question of innovation goes beyond highbacks. Every year, we see a plethora of new lacing systems paraded as the next big thing in snowboarding boots. From traditional laces to quick-pull systems, from Boa® dials to hybrid models combining various methods, the industry is abuzz with options. These innovations, while offering convenience and a degree of customization, often feel like iterative updates rather than groundbreaking improvements. The real question is: what's next? Where's the innovation that fundamentally changes how we interact with our gear?

One innovation, conspicuously absent yet potentially transformative, is a walk mode in snowboarding boots. This feature, a staple in ski touring boots, would be revolutionary for split boarders and backcountry riders. Imagine the ease of ascent, the comfort during long treks, and the versatility it would bring. As a ski boot fitter and an avid snowboarder, I see a significant gap in our boot technology. We've honed in on refining fit and improving lacing systems, but we've yet to take the leap into integrating a walk mode – an innovation that could redefine backcountry snowboarding.

CHAPTER EIGHTEEN:
THE CONUNDRUM OF
SPLITBOARDING
GEAR AND SKI BOOT
TOURING BOOTS

As I dove deeper into the world of splitboarding, I was struck by a glaring paradox in the design of our gear. The more I think about it, the more it baffles me. We have these incredible ski touring boots, designed with a walk mode that allows for backward flexion, making the uphill trek more manageable and comfortable. Yet, when it comes to splitboarding, we're faced with a contradictory setup – bindings with highbacks, completely counterintuitive to the very function of a walk mode.

Let's unpack this. In ski touring, the walk mode is a game-changer. It enables the boot cuff to unlock, allowing the ankle to flex naturally backward, facilitating a walking motion that's essential for climbing slopes. It's a feature that acknowledges the dual nature of backcountry skiing – the ascent and the descent. But then, we turn to splitboarding, where the ascent is equally significant, and we're met with a puzzling scenario. Our bindings, crucial for the downhill ride, come with highbacks that limit ankle movement, effectively negating the benefits of a walk mode, should our boots have one.

This contradiction is more than just a design flaw; it's a fundamental oversight in understanding the splitboarding experience. It's as if the gear is caught in an identity crisis, unsure whether it's aiding the ascent or preparing for the descent. And this brings me to a moment of both excitement and frustration. Why haven't we seen a splitboarding boot with a true walk mode, akin to that of ski touring boots? A boot that genuinely caters to the unique demands of splitboarding – the uphill struggle and the rewarding descent.

And here's where the frustration peaks. Imagine if we had splitboarding boots with an efficient walk mode, only to have a highback on the binding negate that feature. It's akin to taking one step forward and two steps back. The highback, a component initially designed for heel-side support and responsiveness, becomes an obstacle in the very environment it's supposed to excel in.

Moreover, let's address the notion of "heel side edge responsiveness." Yes, it's important, but let's not overestimate the highback's role in this. Our feet are strapped down securely; when you initiate a turn, your toes lift, and the board responds. This isn't the highback's doing – it's basic mechanics facilitated by well-designed straps and boots. And in the context of splitboarding, especially in softer snow conditions like powder, the necessity for extreme heel side responsiveness diminishes. The terrain demands a different approach, one that prioritizes float and maneuverability over aggressive edge control.

This chapter is not just an observation; it's a call for innovation and rethinking. It's an invitation for manufacturers to step back and reconsider the splitboarding setup. Why not develop a boot that truly embraces the essence of splitboarding – a boot with a functional walk mode, designed to work harmoniously with the binding system? A system where the uphill and downhill gear components complement each other rather than work at odds.

As a passionate snowboarder and a ski boot fitter, I've seen the potential for innovation firsthand. The technology exists; it's the application and integration that need reimagining. The dream is a splitboarding boot that mirrors the efficiency of ski touring boots in walk mode, paired with a binding system that respects and enhances this functionality.

In closing, I circle back to the core of snowboarding – it's about freedom, about experiencing the mountain in its purest form. As we continue to evolve in our sport, let's not be afraid to question the status quo. Let's strive for gear that not only meets our needs but elevates our experience. The mountains are calling, and our gear should be an extension of our desire to explore, to ascend, and to descend with grace and ease. It's time for a new chapter in splitboarding gear – one that truly understands and caters to the soul of the backcountry adventurer.

… And let's be unequivocally clear about this glaring contradiction: ski boots' walk mode is ingeniously designed for backward flexion, enhancing the ascent in ski touring. Meanwhile, we splitboarders, perplexingly, are saddled with highbacks during our ascent. This setup is a puzzling contradiction. On one hand, ski touring boots acknowledge and facilitate the natural walking motion essential for uphill travel. On the other, splitboarding bindings, with their highbacks, seem to do the exact opposite, imposing a restriction that seems counterproductive to the very essence of backcountry ascent. So, the burning question remains: Which direction are we truly heading in our gear design for splitboarding? Are we facilitating the ascent, or are we inadvertently hindering it?

**CHAPTER NINETEEN:
THE DAY IN OREGON**

The morning air at Timberline Lodge was crisp and invigorating, a perfect prelude to a day on the slopes. Alex and I stood over garbage cans, methodically scraping the wax off our boards, a ritual marking the transition from the end of the season in Colorado to the beginning of new adventures on Mount Hood.

As I worked, my gaze fell on my bindings. They were among the finest in the market, boasting carbon fiber in both the heel cup and the highback. These bindings, with just a few rides under their belt, were about to be tested in the terrain park of Timberline. I felt a mix of excitement and pride; they represented the cutting edge of snowboarding technology, and I was eager to see how they would perform.

Amidst the scraping of wax, a thought struck me. Why not adjust the forward lean on my bindings? I wanted a more aggressive stance, a low, athletic posture that would allow me to lean into my turns with more force. I was an aggressive rider, always pushing the limits, and I believed that a stiffer stance would enhance my control and responsiveness.

Alex, ever the voice of reason, questioned the necessity of such an adjustment. "I don't see the point," he argued, but I was resolute. I wanted to test the boundaries of my equipment and my abilities. Adjusting the forward lean on my highbacks seemed like a logical step in that direction.

Our day continued, filled with the typical excitement and challenges of a day on the mountain. I was hyper-aware of my bindings, feeling the increased tension in my calves as I leaned into each turn, appreciating the extra support they provided.

It's important to clarify that this is not a chapter of blame or regret.

Yes, my bindings, particularly the decision to increase the forward lean, played a role in the story that unfolded later that day. But they were not the sole factor in the accident that would soon befall me.

Snowboarding, like any adventure sport, comes with its inherent risks, and my experience that day was a harsh reminder of that reality.

As I reflect on that day and the journey that followed, I've come to realize that highbacks, stiff or otherwise, are not a necessity in snowboarding. Risks are an inherent part of our sport, with or without highbacks. But as I learned, combining forward lean with stiff highbacks while launching off big jumps can be a precarious endeavor.

CHAPTER TWENTY:
STRAPPING IN:
THE ESSENCE OF
SNOWBOARDING

In the heart of snowboarding lies a simple yet profound act: strapping in. It's a ritual that transcends the mere action of securing ourselves to the board. Nicholas Mueller, in Nike's "Never Not Part 2," captured this essence with his words: "The one trick is to just strap in." This statement, seemingly straightforward, resonates with a deeper truth about our sport and our lives.

As we age, the act of strapping in becomes more than just a physical undertaking; it evolves into a symbol of perseverance, passion, and commitment. I've witnessed phenomenal skiers and riders, for whom the mountains were a canvas of expression, gradually drift away from the slopes. It's a story that unfolds in various ways - some due to the blessings and responsibilities of life, like starting a family or career growth, others due to the hardships and distractions that life can unexpectedly throw our way.

In ski towns, I've seen how life's complexities can overshadow the very reason people are drawn to these majestic landscapes. For some, the pursuit of the high that skiing and snowboarding provide leads down a path of substance abuse, a quest to replicate the exhilaration of the slopes. This struggle is a stark reminder of the unique wiring of those who are drawn to action sports. We are a different breed, not entirely in sync with the conventional norms and expectations of society.

Those of us who find solace and identity in action sports often resonate more with the laws of nature than the laws of man. The concepts of motion, gravity, and natural terrain make more sense to us than rigid human rules and logic. We find a sense of belonging and understanding in the rhythm of the mountains, the flow of the snow beneath our boards.

But amidst these reflections, it's crucial to circle back to Mueller's insight. His perspective on the 'one trick' of snowboarding isn't just about the physical act of securing the bindings. It's about the commitment to step onto the board, to face the mountain, to embrace the challenges and joys that come with each ride. Strapping in symbolizes the choice to engage with the world in a way that is meaningful and fulfilling to us.

As life progresses, the moments we get to spend on the slopes may become rarer, making them all the more precious. For those living in ski towns, the irony can be stark – surrounded by the very landscapes that define their passion, yet often unable to partake in them as frequently as they'd like. It's a reminder of the importance of cherishing each opportunity to ride, to feel the snow, to be in that moment of pure connection with nature.

So, as we consider the evolution of snowboarding gear, the debates around highbacks, and the innovation in the sport, let's not lose sight of the core of our passion. It's in the simple act of strapping in where our journey begins. Each time we do, we're embracing not just a sport, but a way of life – a choice to pursue what gives us a sense of freedom and joy.

Nicholas Mueller's words resonate as a profound reminder: amid the complexities of life and the ever-changing world of snowboarding, the most significant trick we ever perform is the decision to strap in. It's a choice that defines us, a choice to pursue our passion, to connect with the mountains, and to be true to ourselves. Let's keep riding, keep pushing the boundaries, and most importantly, let's never forget to cherish the simple joy of strapping in and embarking on our next adventure down the mountain.

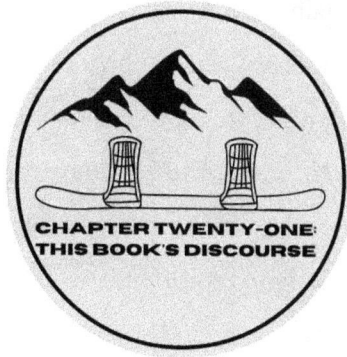

CHAPTER TWENTY-ONE:
THIS BOOK'S DISCOURSE

In the ever-evolving world of snowboarding, each turn on the mountain reflects not just our physical journey but also our choices and changes in life. This book's discourse is a testament to that evolution, highlighting the privilege of choice and discussion in our sport. The journey back to the slopes, especially as life unfolds with its myriad challenges, can be a formidable one. Yet, in those moments when we hear the click of our bindings, we're reminded of the essence of snowboarding - a sport that embodies freedom, expression, and connection with the natural world.

Snowboarding, like life, is a narrative filled with twists, turns, and unexpected leaps. Through the pages of this book, we've traversed snowboarding's rich history, observing how highbacks, once revolutionary, have now entered a phase where their necessity is questioned. The advancements in snowboarding gear, particularly boots and bindings, have created new dynamics in how we interact with our boards and the mountain.

We've outgrown certain aspects of our gear just as we outgrow phases in our lives. Our journey with highbacks has been enlightening, but as we move forward, it's essential to evaluate their role in modern snowboarding. The current state of technology, with sophisticated straps and heel cups, provides us with the control and connection that highbacks were initially designed to offer. This evolution prompts us to consider whether highbacks are an indispensable component or a remnant of the past that we can gracefully let go.

As snowboarders, we're constantly pushing boundaries, seeking to improve and adapt. This journey isn't about disregarding our past but about understanding and embracing progression. Highbacks have been fundamental in shaping snowboarding, but as the sport matures, our gear must evolve too. This evolution isn't a one-size-fits-all approach. Some riders may continue to prefer highbacks, valuing their familiarity.

Snowboarding has always been about more than just the equipment; it's about the experiences, the connections, and the memories we create on and off the slopes.

As we bring this book to a conclusion, we find ourselves on the cusp of yet another new era in snowboarding. It seems this sport is in a constant state of evolution, and we are privileged to be both spectators and active contributors in its unfolding journey.

The mountain before us is vast, with uncharted paths and fresh opportunities. Whether we choose to ride with highbacks or venture into new territories without them, the essence of our journey remains the same. It's about embracing the thrill of the ride, the beauty of the mountains, and the freedom that comes with carving our path.

So, as we end this chapter and look towards the future, let's remember that the most significant 'trick' in snowboarding is the joy of strapping in and experiencing the mountain in our unique way. Whether you're a seasoned rider or new to the slopes, this is a call to explore, to experiment, and to continue writing our own stories on the snow.

Let's embrace the future of snowboarding with open hearts and minds. Let's ride, explore, and continue to push the boundaries of what's possible. The slopes await, and our next adventure is just a binding click away.

**AN UNSEEN VARIABLE:
THE EPILOGUE**

As I sat on my childhood bed in New Jersey in 2013, with Sheena, my loyal black lab, resting beside me, a forgotten memory from the morning of my accident at Mount Hood came crashing back. It was a moment of revelation, a critical piece of the puzzle I hadn't realized was missing until now.

I remembered waking up that fateful morning, greeted by the stunning beauty of Oregon's peaks. Alex was already up, a fire crackling and a Bloody Mary in hand. "Good morning, my dude!" he had called out cheerfully. "Do you want a bloody?"

"Good morning, bro!" I had replied, feeling the anticipation of the day's ride. "Hell yeah, I do. I'm going to go take a shit first."

"In the woods?" Alex inquired, a hint of humor in his voice.

"I'm going to see if the lodge is open." I had decided, seeking the comfort of indoor facilities.

"Take my skateboard," Alex suggested, offering a quicker return from the lodge. A nod to our shared love of anything on wheels.

The lodge was indeed open. After attending to nature's call, I left, hopping onto Alex's skateboard for the ride back down the parking lot. The lot was not steep, but it was long, and before I knew it, I was gaining more speed than I had anticipated. Smiling and waving to fellow early risers, my heart swelled with the camaraderie shared among those who make their temporary homes in these makeshift lots. RVs, buses, vans, and sedans with grills and beers – a village of adventurers greeting the day.

Soon, however, I realized the need to slow down. The familiar feel of a skateboard under my feet gave way to the unfamiliar response of Alex's longboard. I attempted to brake as I usually would, but the longboard had other plans. As the speed wobbles began, my calm mind contrasted with the quickening pace of my heart.

Aiming for the snowpack at the end of the lot, I made a last-minute decision to bail. Jumping off the skateboard, I took several long, adrenaline-fueled strides before tumbling into the snow. Picking myself up, my shins throbbed with a pain that I initially shrugged off.

Hobbling back to the campsite, Bloody Mary in hand, I sat next to Alex and Sheena, overlooking the magnificent landscape. "Fuck, dude. I think I may have just given myself shin splints or something. I fucked my shins up hopping of your board in the lot," I confessed.

"Still good to ride?" Alex had asked, concern lacing his voice.

"Of course, my guy. Of course."

That incident, which I had initially brushed off as a minor inconvenience, was now a significant element in the story of my accident. It was a critical factor, an unseen variable that contributed to the catastrophic break on Mount Hood.

This revelation reshaped my understanding of that day. It wasn't just about the jump or the landing, nor was it solely about the highbacks or the gear. It was also about the condition in which I had approached the slopes – already compromised, yet unaware of how profoundly it would affect the outcome.

In that moment of clarity, I recognized the importance of acknowledging every factor in our journeys, whether on the slopes or in life. We often focus on the most apparent elements, overlooking the subtleties that can have profound impacts. My experience serves as a reminder of the interconnectedness of our actions, decisions, and circumstances.

As I reflect on this, I am reminded of the importance of being mindful and aware, of listening to our bodies and our instincts. This epilogue isn't just a conclusion to a story of an injury; it's an insight into the complex tapestry of factors that define our experiences. It's a testament to the need for a holistic perspective, one that considers all variables, seen and unseen.

In the end, every rider's journey is unique, filled with its own challenges and lessons. Mine has been a journey of discovery, resilience, and growth. It's a story shared with every snowboarder who has ever faced the unexpected, who has navigated the unpredictable terrain of both the mountains and life. And it's a story that continues, with each new dawn, each new ride, and each new lesson learned along the way.

… Oh yeah, and highbacks aren't a necessity. They're a choice.

Dear Reader,

As I pen this note, the journey of writing this book comes to a close, but the adventure it represents is just beginning. The pages you've just turned are not just filled with words, but with pieces of my heart, soul, and the undying spirit of snowboarding.

I want to express my deepest gratitude to you for choosing to embark on this narrative adventure. Your support is not just about reading a book; it's about sharing a passion, a love for the slopes, and an appreciation for the ever-evolving world of snowboarding.

As an independent author, your feedback means the world to me. It's the fuel that keeps the fire of creativity and storytelling burning. If you found joy, insight, or even a moment of reflection in this book, I would be deeply honored if you could take a few minutes to leave a review. Your thoughts, opinions, and experiences are invaluable, not just to me, but to other readers who share our passion for the mountains and the thrill of the ride.

Your reviews help in sharing this story with a wider audience and in continuing the conversation about the evolution and essence of snowboarding. They also provide me with essential insights and inspiration as I continue on my journey as a writer and a snowboarder.

Thank you once again for your time, your spirit, and your love for the snow. May your trails be ever adventurous, your rides thrilling, and your connections with nature profound. Here's to many more days of carving slopes and creating memories!

Keep riding and stay safe.

With heartfelt gratitude,
Nitka Marga

P.S. Remember, the greatest trick in snowboarding is the joy of strapping in. Let's keep sharing our stories and pushing the boundaries together.